A MUSICAL FOR CHILDREN ABOUT THE POWER OF GOD

Created by Pam Andrews

Arranged by John DeVries

LILLENAS
PUBLISHING COMPANY

lillenas.com

Contents

Cast

NARRATOR

RANGER CLARK / CAPTAIN SUPER

NED / BIBLE BOY WONDER

SHARK

SNAKE

GANG OF GOLIATHS

TYLER

CARL

JAMES

JENNA

TORI

DAVID

ESTHER

JOSEPH

JOSHUA

Overture
Joshua Fought the Battle of Jericho

Traditional
Arr. by John DeVries

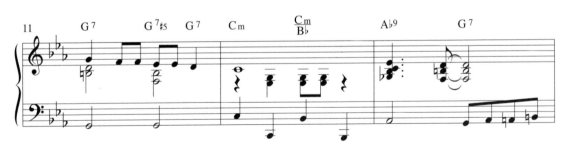

NARRATOR *(stage left)*: This is the city…or should I say…city park also known as Hero Park. The kids from Trinity Church are arriving for their annual camp out as we speak. *(music begins)* What questions are lurking in the shadows? What dangers are approaching? Listen and learn as you meet the first action heroes…coming to save the day.

(Kids enter as song begins. They are wearing First Action Hero T-shirts and capes.)

The First Action Hero

Words and Music by
PAM ANDREWS
Arr. by John DeVries

13

Com-ing to bring__ the world__ good news,__ com-ing to show__ the way.__

He's the first ac - tion He - ro, He is

pow-er, He is__ true blue.__ Look, here He comes__ to save__

the day,__ Je - sus, our He - ro is

CD: 7 *3rd time*

3rd time to Coda
(to pg. 11, meas. 46)

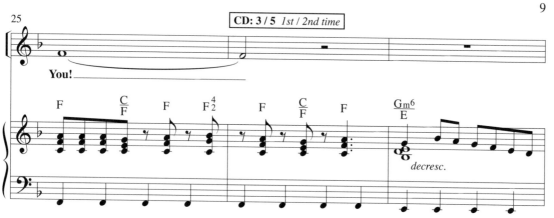

CD: 3 / 5 *1st / 2nd time*

You!_____

1. Je - sus brings_ us pow - er,
2. Je - sus is_____ our He - ro,

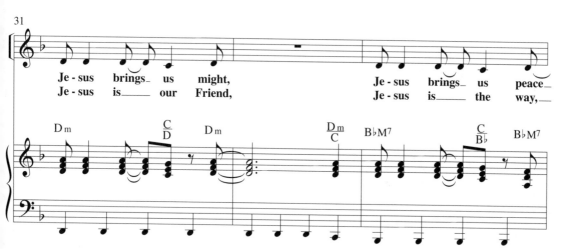

Je - sus brings_ us might,   Je - sus brings_ us peace_
Je - sus is_____ our Friend,   Je - sus is_____ the way, _

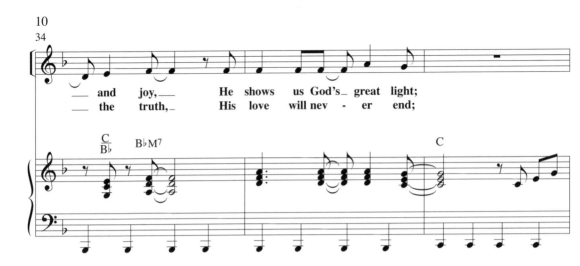

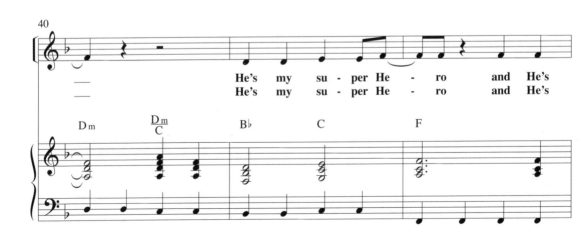

1st time: D.S.   11
2nd time: D.S. al Coda
(to pg. 7, meas. 9)

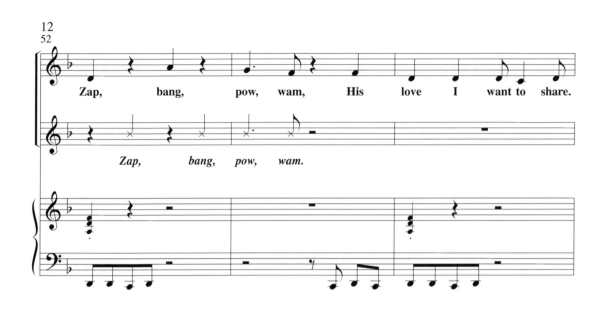

Zap, bang, pow, wam, His love I want to share.

Zap, bang, pow, wam.

Zap, bang, pow, wam,

Zap, bang, pow, wam.

Mas - ter, Lead-er true. You're my He - ro,

ALL

C   Dm7/C

CD: 8

You're my Lord,__ I give my life to You.__

He's the first ac - tion He -

- ro com-ing to save__ the day,__

Com - ing to bring__ the world__ good news,__

SCENE 1

(The stage begins dim. The drama kids enter the scene with flashlights and shine them out to the audience as they move to center stage. They are carrying back packs and sleeping bags.)

JAMES: Hey, everyone, this looks like the spot.

CARL: Ranger Clark told us to look for the First Action Hero exhibit.

TYLER: I guess this is it. Cool!

TORI: These giant comic books are awesome.

JENNA: Where's my bug repellent? *(scratches her arm)* I'm already dinner for a mosquito.

(kids continue setting up camp as the narrator speaks)

NARRATOR: Rapidly approaching are Ranger Clark and Ned. Little did they know that this would be a night they would remember.

(NED enters the camp)

NED: Welcome everyone to the Trinity Church Camp Out at Hero Park. This is gonna be a wonderful night of fun and excitement. *(pause)* Now, kids, here is the magnificent leader of our Hero celebration, Ranger Clark.

(Clark enters stage right)

ALL KIDS *(clapping)*: Yea!

RANGER: Hey kids. This is gonna to be a wonderful night. Learning about some of the first Bible action heroes will be super. Okay, campers finish stowing your gear and let's make camp.

(kids begin to place their sleeping bags on stage and pretend to establish a campsite)

Goliaths' Theme (Entrance)

PAM ANDREWS and
JOHN DEVRIES
Arr. by John DeVries

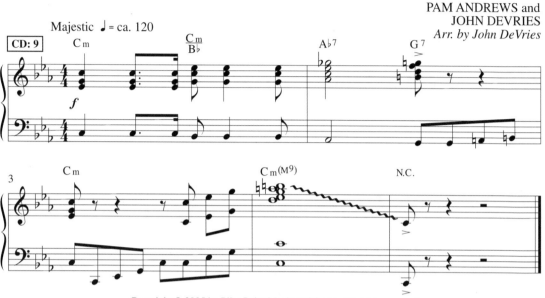

(The GOLIATHS enter stage right and begin lurking behind trees. They are dressed in gang style clothes and carrying spray paint cans. The GOLIATHS consist of SHARK and SNAKE and as many other Goliath gang members that you choose.)

NARRATOR: Meanwhile…nearby…lurking in the shadows are those evildoers from the local school…the Goliaths.

(GOLIATHS remain hidden until RANGER CLARK and NED exit)

RANGER: Ned, did you bring logs for the fire?

NED: No, I thought you put the wood in the truck.

RANGER: Nope. Sometimes I think I would forget my head if it weren't attached. Okay, kids, looks like we're in need of some firewood. Ned and I will be back shortly. *(to NED as they exit stage right)*

Goliaths' Theme (Underscore)

PAM ANDREWS and
JOHN DEVRIES
Arr. by John DeVries

(SHARK and SNAKE and the gang of GOLIATHS slither toward center stage. SHARK speaks to TYLER.)

SHARK: Hey dude. What do ya think you're doin'?

TYLER: Are you talkin' to me?

SHARK: Yeah. I'm talkin' to you.

TORI: Don't I know you? Don't you go to our school?

SHARK: Yeah, right. I'm Shark and this is Snake and this is our gang, the Goliaths.

JENNA: I thought you were Albert Thompson and Ernest Jones.

CARL *(laughingly)*: Yeah, get a load of Bert and Ernie!

SNAKE *(looks angrily at CARL)*: I think I asked you a question. Why are you here? This area of the park is off limits to dweebs like you.

JAMES *(nervously)*: Um…We're here for the Trinity Church Camp Out.

SNAKE *(to James)*: Hey, aren't you that wimpy kid from school?

SHARK: Weren't you the kid we stuffed in the locker?

(GOLIATHS laugh)

TYLER: Hey, cut it out.

(TYLER pats JAMES on the back. JAMES looks down as if embarrassed.)

SHARK *(walks to the comic book cover exhibit)*: Snake, get a load of these comic book covers. They're beggin' for some Goliath graffiti. *(holds up a spray paint can.)*

TORI: Oh, no. Please don't.

JENNA: Please, just leave us alone.

SHARK: Just in case you wimps don't know, this is Goliath turf. You dudes need to take a hike.

TYLER *(courageously)*: Move…I don't think so…*(SNAKE holds up his fist and TYLER changes his mind)* On second thought…everyone, get your gear and let's go.

(kids scramble to their gear)

Goliaths' Theme (Exit)

PAM ANDREWS and
JOHN DEVRIES
Arr. by John DeVries

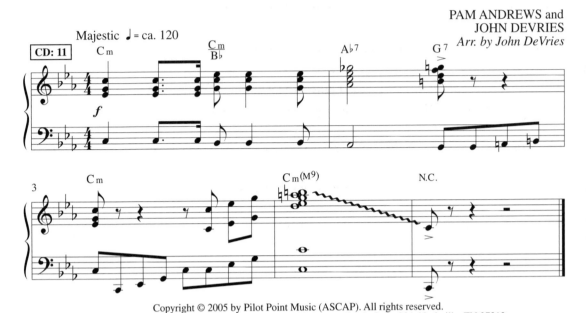

SNAKE: And remember…we'll be watching you!

GOLIATHS: Yeah. We'll be watchin' you.

(GOLIATHS exit stage right)

JAMES: I guess that's our cue to hit the road.

(kids begin gathering their things)

NARRATOR: What were the campers to do? Stay and face the wrath of the Goliaths or move on to another campsite? Little did they know that help was on the way.

TYLER: Come on everyone, get your stuff.

JAMES: Yeah, we don't want to mess with the Goliaths.

JENNA: They're so scary.

CARL: But, if we move now, how will Ned and Ranger Clark find us?

TORI: Right, Carl. Maybe we should stay until they get back.

TYLER: Good idea.

CARL: You guys know what Ranger Clark would tell us to do…He would want us to talk to
God about our situation. Come on, everyone, let's pray. *(kids bow their heads)*
"Lord, please help us. We're afraid! We need Your power, Lord. Help Ranger Clark
and Ned to get back soon. We love You and thank You for what You're gonna do.
Amen." *(yawns)* It's getting late. Let's go ahead and camp here. Just remember,
Jesus is with us! Come on everyone, let's hit the sack.

(kids begin getting into their sleeping bags)

KIDS: Good night! Yeah, Good night everybody.

(kids get in their sleeping bags and several pull their covers over their heads)

Action Heroes' Theme (Entrance)

PAM ANDREWS
Arr. by John DeVries

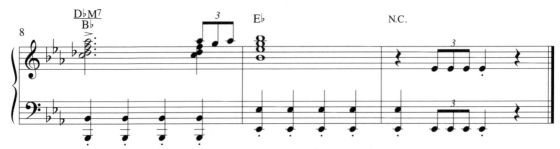

NARRATOR: Never fear…the Lord is near. As the kids curl up in their sleeping bags, the Lord sends them a message…a wonderful message from heaven. Help is on the way.

(Smoke appears from behind the comic book covers. The ACTION HEROES have entered from behind the city landscape to position themselves behind their comic book pages. Ranger Clark and NED reappear as super heroes CAPTAIN SUPER and the BIBLE BOY WONDER from behind the Jesus page. DAVID, ESTHER, JOSEPH, and JOSHUA come from behind their respective comic book pages.)

CAPTAIN SUPER: Here we come to show the way!

BIBLE BOY WONDER: Captain Super, remember your blood pressure.

(Kids jump up in surprise and fear. They nervously huddle together stage left.)

TYLER: Who are you?

CAPTAIN SUPER: We're the First Action Heroes coming to show you the way. I'm Captain Super and this is Bible Boy Wonder.

BIBLE BOY WONDER: Hey kids!

KIDS *(hesitantly)*:Hey! Hey, Dude! Hello!

CAPTAIN SUPER: And these are the First Action Heroes.

(each ACTION HERO steps forward as they are introduced)

CAPTAIN SUPER: This is David, the super hero of trust; Esther, the super hero of courage; Joseph, the super hero of forgiveness; and Joshua, the super hero of obedience. Finally, we will introduce you to the most important Action Hero…the Hero above all Heroes …Jesus. We have come to help you on your quest for power…the power that comes only from God.

(music begins)

Quest for Power

Words and Music by
PAM ANDREWS
Arr. by John DeVries

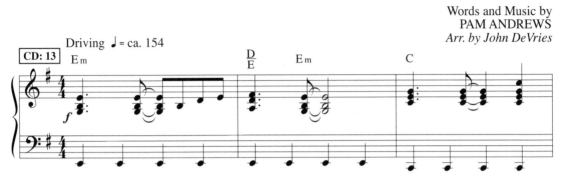

21

Ac - tion He - roes one_____ and all, We're

23

on a quest for pow - er._____

26 CD: 14 / 16 *1st / 2nd time*

29 SOLO Captain Super Hero

mf

1. Let me in - tro - duce_____ to you
2. Da - vid had_____ the pow'r_____ to trust

He - roes who___ are tried___ and true, For
Es - ther's cour - age was___ a must, For -

they knew just___ what they___ should do When
give - ness Jo - seph showed___ to us What

things were look - in' bad___ They would look___ to God___
pow - er, what___ great might,___ Jos - hua told___ us to___

SCENE 2

TORI *(to DAVID)*: Are you sure you're not a Goliath?

DAVID: Not hardly. I took care of him a long time ago.

BIBLE BOY WONDER: We heard that you were in need of our assistance so as quick as a flash *(makes quick hand gestures)* …zap, pow, blast…Here we are!

CAPTAIN SUPER: Tell me about the Goliaths…who are these creatures?

TYLER: "Creatures" is a good word for them. They're this gang at school that tries to bully the rest of us.

TORI: They push kids around and make fun of how we look.

James: Yeah…they really did put me in my locker once.

JENNA: They're simply horrible.

CARL: They were here a little while ago. They told us that this was their turf and that we had to move.

CAPTAIN SUPER: Sounds like a tough situation. We would love to provide you our assistance. Let's power up, Action Heroes.

Action Heroes' Theme (Underscore)

PAM ANDREWS
Arr. by John DeVries

(They put their hands together in the center of a circle as if a sports team.)

ACTION HEROES: God's Power up!

BIBLE BOY WONDER: The Bible is full of answers, kids. Let's see what this wonderful book has to say about your situation. *(reads from the Bible)* "Trust in the LORD with all your heart and lean not on your own understanding." Proverbs 3:5.

DAVID: Let me see if I can help. *(moves center stage to tell his story)*

DAVID: My name is David. I, too had a bully problem whose name was Goliath. In fact, he was bullying all of Israel's army.

TYLER: I heard about your story at Sunday School. The Philistines and the Israelites were at war.

JENNA: Yes, and Goliath was a warrior in the Philistine camp.

JAMES: Was he really over nine feet tall?

DAVID: Yes, believe me, that Goliath was a real giant! He yelled at the Israelite camp, "Choose a man and have him come fight me."

CARL: What happened next?

DAVID: Well, I was at the camp bringing bread to my older brothers when I heard Goliath's threats. I went to King Saul and volunteered to fight the giant.

TORI: How could you volunteer to fight such a giant?

DAVID: I trusted God. As I approached Goliath, he laughed at my size, but I said, "I come against you in the name of the LORD Almighty." I placed a small stone in my sling, and God guided it right to the giant's forehead! God helped me trust Him and gave Israel the victory!

CAPTAIN SUPER: That's a great story, David. Trust is an awesome power.

(music begins)

Trust Is a Must

Words and Music by
PAM ANDREWS and
PAM WALKER
Arr. by John DeVries

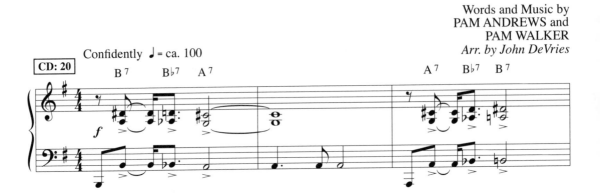

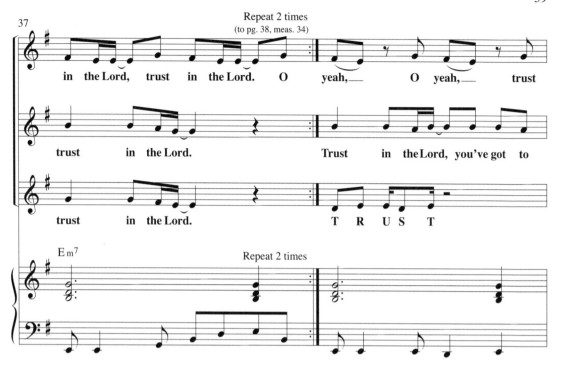

CD: 24

SCENE 3

JAMES (*rocking his hands in front of him in a circle*): I'm trustin', I'm trustin', yeah, yeah, I'm trustin'.

TORI: Cool it, James.

BIBLE BOY WONDER: The Bible says in 1 Corinthians 16:13, "Be on your guard; stand firm in the faith; be men of courage; be strong."

CAPTAIN SUPER: Esther, your story might help them understand.

ESTHER (*steps to center stage*): When I was a girl, I lived with my cousin, Mordecai, after my parents died. We were Jews who were captives in Persia. One day, I was chosen by King Xerxes to become his wife.

TORI: That's because you're so pretty.

ESTHER: Why, thank you, Tori.

JAMES: Didn't Mordecai warn you to never tell the King you're a Jew?

ESTHER: Yes. Unfortunately, a noble of the King, named Hamen, wanted to destroy the Jews.

CARL: Why did he not like the Jews?

ESTHER: We were different. Sadly, the King agreed to this terrible plan. Mordecai found out about the plot; and told me, "Esther, you must go before the King and persuade him to spare the Jews." I knew I was risking my life because anyone who approached the King without permission would be put to death.

JENNA: I would be so afraid.

ESTHER: The only exception to this fate was for the king to extend his golden scepter sparing the person's life.

ESTHER: For three days, Mordecai and I, along with all the other Jews fasted and prayed. As I approached the King, I asked God for courage to do what He wanted me to do.

TYLER: What did the king do, Esther?

ESTHER: When the King saw me, he extended his scepter giving me permission to speak. I asked him to come to a banquet I was preparing for him and bring Hamen with him. They came and ate with me, and I invited them back to eat the next day. The King asked, "Queen Esther, what do you want?" I said, "O King, spare my life and spare my people. The Jews have been ordered to destruction by Hamen." So the King changed the proclamation and saved my people...the Jews. God gave me the courage to face the King and possible death.

CAPTAIN SUPER: Yes, kids, to conquer your fears, God will give you courage. (*music begins*)

Courage Conquers Fear

PAM WALKER, LINDA COULTER
and PAM ANDREWS

RANDLE MOORE, JOHN DEVRIES
and PAM ANDREWS
Arr. by John DeVries

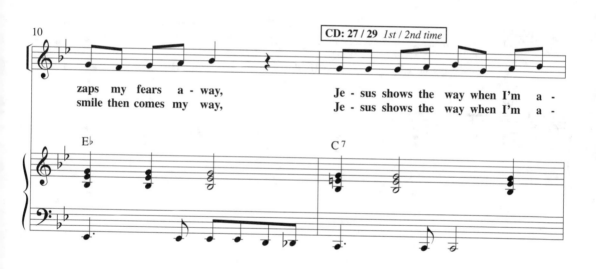

Je - sus near, He whis - pers in your heart, "Please know I'm

al - ways here." He'll give to you His pow - er, hear His

mes - sage clear. Just face it, own it,

GROUP 1

GROUP 2

Face it, own it,

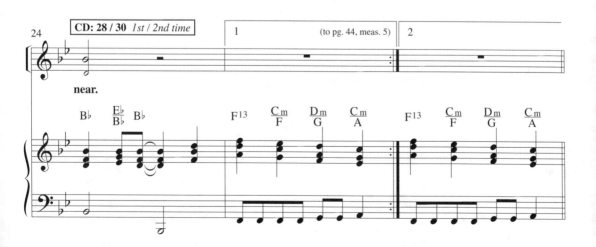

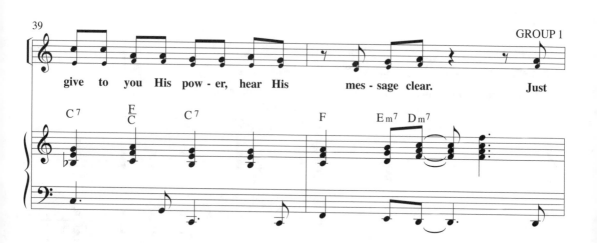

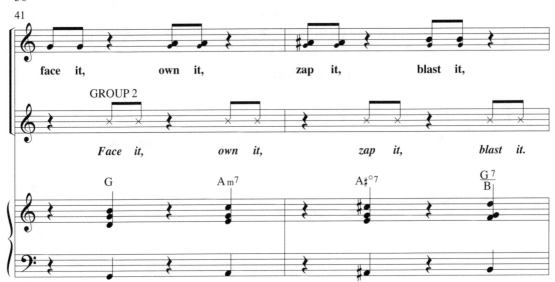

face it, own it, zap it, blast it,

GROUP 2

Face it, own it, zap it, blast it.

Cour - age con - quers fear with Je - sus near.

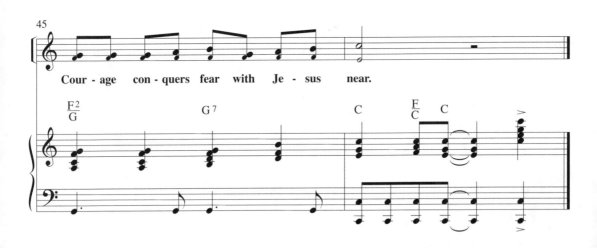

Cour - age con - quers fear with Je - sus near.

SCENE 4

JENNA: Are you saying we should fight the Goliaths?

TORI: Fighting doesn't seem to be the right answer.

CAPTAIN SUPER: Truthfully, God wants you to forgive.

BIBLE BOY WONDER: Let's see what the Bible says about forgiveness. Colossians 3:13 says, "Bear with each other and forgive whatever grievances you may have against one another. Forgive as the Lord forgave you."

JAMES: How can I forgive those dudes for stuffing me in that locker?

TYLER: Forgive the Goliaths?

CARL: No way!

JOSEPH: I can teach you about forgiveness. My name is Joseph and I'm next to the last of the sons of Jacob.

CARL: Weren't you your father's favorite son?

JOSEPH: Yes, in fact, he loved me so much, he made me a special coat of many colors. My brothers were very jealous and hated me. One day, they took away my special coat, and sold me into slavery. They told my father I had been killed. I lived as a slave and was placed in a prison for something that I did not do. During this time, Pharaoh, King of Egypt, had some horrible nightmares. God helped me be able to tell him the meaning of his dreams.

TORI: Sometimes, I have bad dreams.

JOSEPH: In Pharaoh's dreams, God was warning of a terrible famine that would soon come to Egypt. Because I could explain the dreams, I was released from prison, made governor, and put in charge of the land of Egypt. The famine spread into Canaan, where my family lived.

JAMES: Doesn't a famine mean there are no crops?

JOSEPH: Yes. My father sent my brothers to Egypt to buy grain. When I saw them, I recognized them, but they did not know me. They came several times to buy grain from me; and on a certain day, I asked them to have dinner with me. At that time, I told them who I was.

JENNA: They must have been so afraid!

JOSEPH: They were terribly afraid, Jenna. They thought that I would kill them because of what they had done to me.

TYLER: What did you do, Joseph?

JOSEPH: I told them, "You meant it for evil, but God meant it for good." God taught me to forgive. When my brothers asked my forgiveness, it was a joyful thing to do.

CAPTAIN SUPER: Forgiveness might be the strongest power of all.

(music begins)

You're Forgiven

Words and Music by
PAM ANDREWS
Arr. by John DeVries

gives and then_ for - gets_ what you_ have done; He ac-

cepts you, you're for - giv - en By the

CD: 33 / 35 *1st / 2nd time*

grace of God_ and by_ His on - ly Son.

SOLO
mf

1. You said a word_ that's wrong,_ a
2. For - give - ness is___ so sweet,_ it

prom - ise you___ for - got
o - pens up___ your heart,

And then you were___ un - kind,___
For - give - ness brings___ friends back___

___ did some - thing you___ should not;___
___ who once___ were far____ a - part;___

Just
For -

pray this sim - ple prayer
give and then___ for - get___

to Je - sus make___ it right,___
and let that an - ger go,___

SCENE 5

BIBLE BOY WONDER: Forgiving others shows you are obeying God. Deuteronomy 27:10 says, "Obey the Lord your God and follow His commands and decrees that I give you today."

JAMES: My mom is always saying, "James Michael Simmons! Obey your mother."

JOSHUA: I learned a long time ago that being obedient to God was one of the most important things anyone can do. *(moves to center stage)* I'm Joshua. All the Israelites had crossed the Jordan under my leadership and entered the land of Canaan. God wanted us to take the land a city at a time, and Jericho was first on the list. When we saw the city, it looked like an impossible task! Jericho had giant walls!

CARL: I read that some of the walls of Jericho were even twelve feet thick!

JENNA: How could you ever get through that wall?

JOSHUA: The Lord's instruction to me was quite clear: "March around the city once with seven priests in front of the Ark, blowing their horns followed by all the armed men. Do this for six days."

JAMES: What a strange way to conquer a city!

JOSHUA: On the seventh day, we did the same thing, but this time we marched around the city seven times. On the seventh time, the priests made a long blast on their horns; and when the people heard the sound, everyone shouted. The Lord caused the walls of the city to fall down and every person went straight into the city to capture it.

CARL: Man, what a cool story.

JOSHUA: I'm sure there were those who questioned God's way. God rewarded our obedience with an unbelievable victory!

CAPTAIN SUPER: By obeying God, you will experience a mighty power like Joshua.

(music begins)

Tell Me What Ya Know About Joshua

with
Joshua Fought the Battle of Jericho

Words and Music by
GARY SIMMONS
Arr. by John DeVries

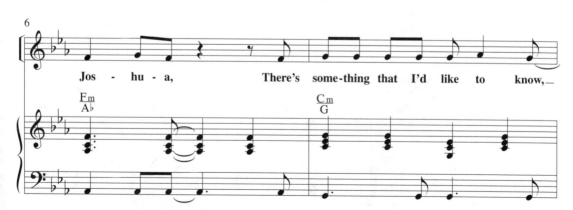

he would need a right hand man;_____ It
mand-ed him to con-quer them;_____ The

did-n't take him long to see that Jos-hu - a would be o -
prob-lem was a wall that was a - round the town that had a

be - di - ent to God's great plan._____ So
gate that would-n't let them in._____ God

af - ter man - y years God knew the time was right to lead His
or - dered him to walk a - round it sev - en times, he did - n't

peo - ple to the prom - ised land;____ The
e - ven try to hes - i - tate;____ With

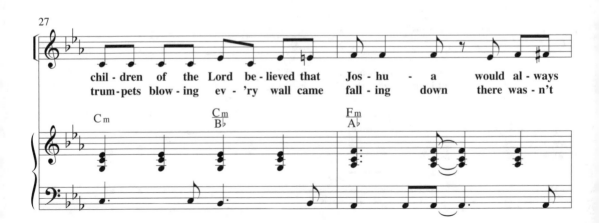

chil - dren of the Lord be - lieved that Jos - hu - a would al - ways
trum - pets blow - ing ev - 'ry wall came fall - ing down there was - n't

1st time: Repeat 65
2nd time: D.S. al Coda
(to pg. 61, meas. 5)

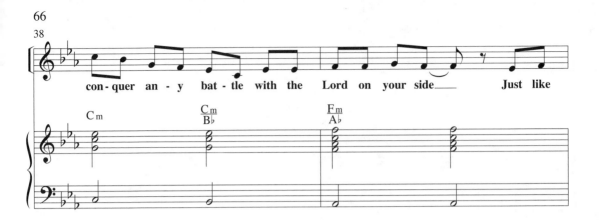

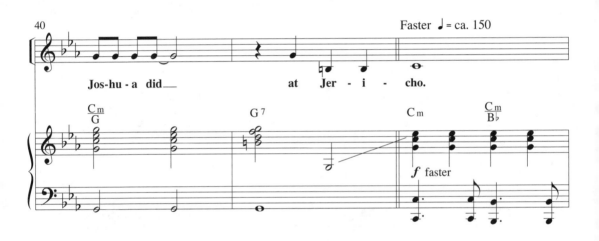

*"Joshua Fought the Battle of Jericho"

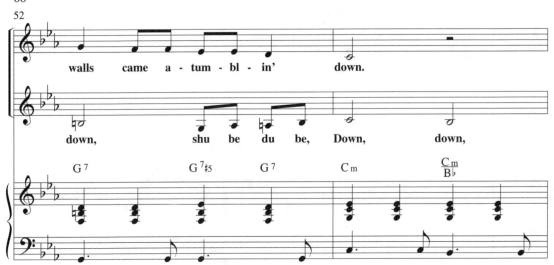

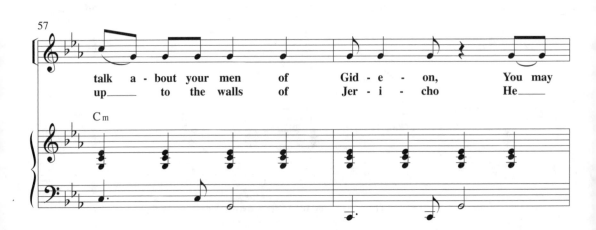

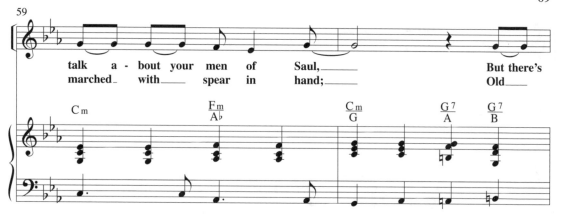

talk a - bout your men of Saul,_____ But there's
marched_ with_____ spear in hand;_____ Old_____

CD: 46 / 47 *1st / 2nd time*

none_____ like_____ good_____ old Jos - hu - a At the
Jos - hu - a com - mand - ed the chil - dren SHOUT And the

1

(to pg. 67, meas. 46)

bat - tle of Jer - i - cho. O

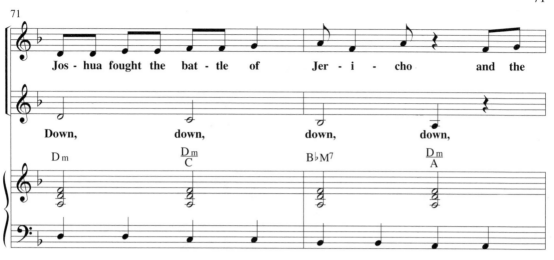

77

a - bout Jos - hu - a,_____

Down, down, down, shu be du be, Down, down,

80

a - bout Jos - hu - a_____ and the

down, shu be du be, Down, down, down, down, and the

83

walls came a - tum - bl - in' down!_____

walls came a - tum - bl - in' down!_____

SCENE 6

TYLER: Trust, courage, forgiveness, and obedience…Is there anything missing, Captain Super?

CAPTAIN SUPER: Yes, you need the power of God's love in your heart.

BIBLE BOY WONDER: 1 John 4:7 says, "Dear friends, let us love one another, for love comes from God. Everyone who loves has been born of God and knows God."

Action Heroes' Theme (Long Underscore)

PAM ANDREWS
Arr. by John DeVries

DAVID: God's Love came to earth in a city called Bethlehem in the form of a little Baby.

ESTHER: God's Love came to earth to teach us how to live. His love heals the sick and helps the hurting.

JOSEPH: God's Love came to earth to make a way for us to know God. The love we are talking about is Jesus, the Son of God…Jesus the Savior of all men. Jesus showed us the love of God when He died on the cross for the sins of the whole world.

JOSHUA: But, God's love did not stop at the tomb. Jesus rose again and is now making us a home in heaven.

JOSHUA: Everyone who receives Him as Lord, receives the love God has to give.

CAPTAIN SUPER: Jesus…He is the Love.

(music begins)

(During the song, CAPTAIN SUPER, Bible Boy Wonder, and the Action Heroes exit behind the comic book pages through the city landscape. They could re-enter the choir or re-appear during the bows at the end of the musical. CAPTAIN SUPER and Bible Boy Wonder change back to RANGER CLARK and NED.)

He Is the Love

Words and Music by
PAM ANDREWS
Arr. by John DeVries

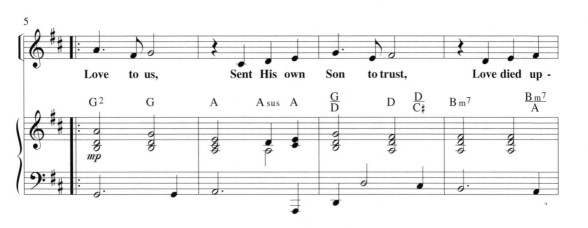

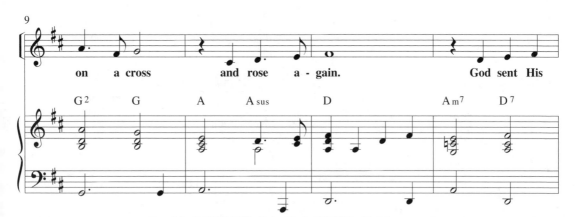

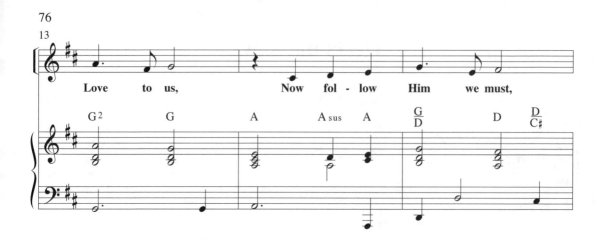

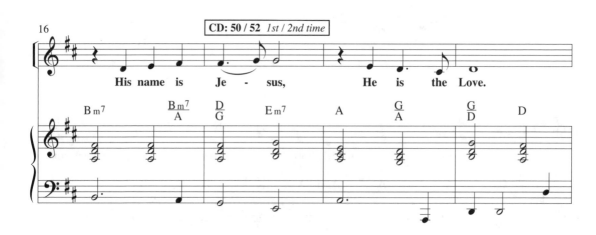

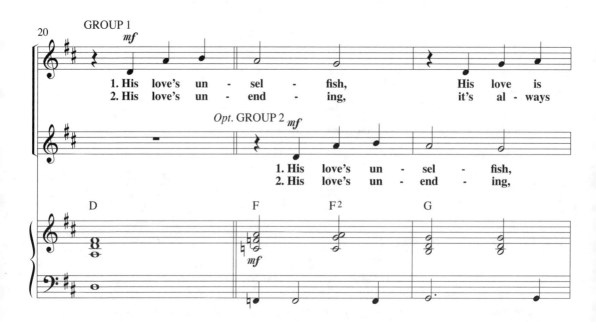

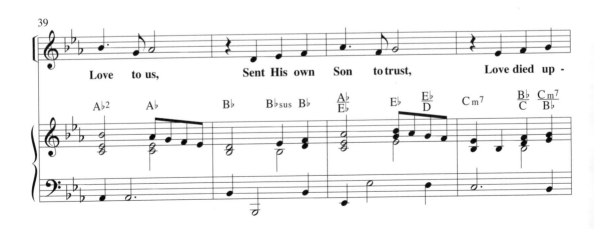

SCENE 7

CARL: Hey, where'd they go?

JENNA: Were we dreaming?

TORI: I don't know.

TYLER: I just know I'm feeling stronger.

JAMES: I'm feelin' the power. *(shows muscles)* I'm not afraid anymore.

(KIDS should move stage left and talk quietly with one another about all they have seen)

ALL KIDS: They're unbelievable! That was amazing! They are so cool! They were awesome!

Goliaths' Theme (Return)

PAM ANDREWS and
JOHN DEVRIES
Arr. by John DeVries

(GOLIATHS enter from stage right carrying spray paint cans)

NARRATOR: Meanwhile, creeping in the shadows are the Goliaths. What will happen next... will the kids fight back with people power or take action with the super powers of God? Watch and learn...

SNAKE: Come on, Shark, let's get busy and add some Goliath art to these signs.

SHARK: Yeah, right.

(GOLIATHS run to the comic book exhibit, but SHARK falls and hurts his ankle)

SHARK: Ouch. Hey, man, this dude is hurt. Goliaths, help me! Snake, come on! Help me!

SNAKE: Forget you...Someone's coming. Come on, Goliaths! We're outta here.

Goliaths' Theme (Final Exit)

PAM ANDREWS and
JOHN DEVRIES
Arr. by John DeVries

PLEASE NOTE: Copying of this product is NOT covered by CCLI licenses. For CCLI information call 1-800-234-2446.

(SNAKE and the GOLIATHS run away, leaving SHARK alone. The kids are suddenly aware someone is hurt.)

TYLER: It's Shark and he's hurt.

JAMES: We need to help him.

CARL: Tyler, you get his other arm. James, you get his leg.

SHARK: Ouch. It's my ankle.

TORI: Here. Put him on this park bench.

JENNA: And he can put his foot on my pillow.

(RANGER CLARK and NED enter in their original costumes from stage right carrying firewood. They drop the firewood and hurry to help the kids with SHARK.)

RANGER: Hey, kids. What's going on?

TORI *(to RANGER CLARK)*: Shark has fallen and hurt his ankle. *(to SHARK)* Don't worry, Shark. We're gonna help you.

(SHARK tries to walk...but stumbles and falls back on the bench in pain.)

SHARK: Ouch! I don't think I can walk.

JENNA: Well, just stay put.

JAMES: Someone get an ice pack for his ankle.

(TORI gets an ice pack from the first aid kit and gives it to SHARK)

SHARK: Why would you guys want to help me?

CARL: Relax, Shark. We're cool.

TORI: I guess you could say we've been powered up by the First Action Hero.

TYLER: Yeah, Shark, we've got the love of God in our hearts ready to share with you. His love is more powerful and can conquer any bad feelings we have toward you. God's love is amazing!

(music begins)

Indescribable

Words and Music by
LAURA STORY
Arr. by John DeVries

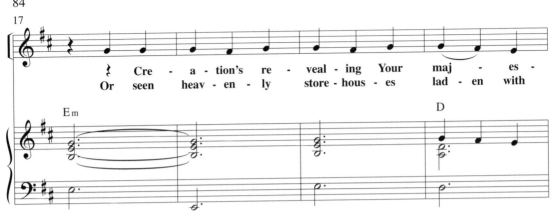

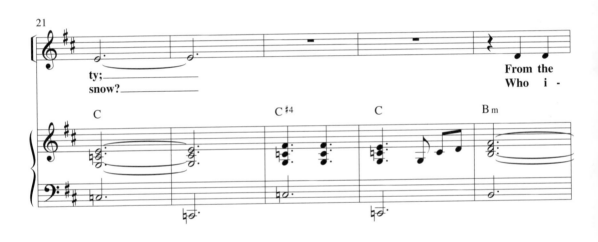

Ev - 'ry crea-ture u -
Yet con - ceals it to

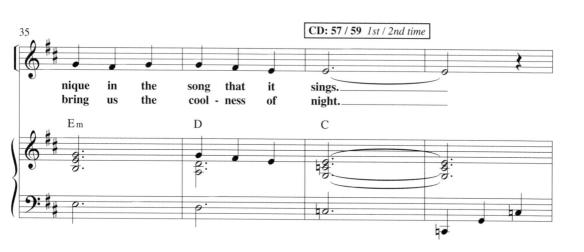

CD: 57 / 59 *1st / 2nd time*

nique in the song that it sings.
bring us the cool - ness of night.

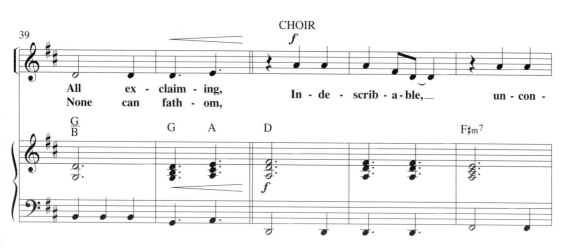

CHOIR

All ex - claim - ing,
None can fath - om,

In - de - scrib - a - ble,— un - con -

fall to our knees as we hum-bly pro - claim,___

You are a - maz - ing___ God.___

(to pg. 83, meas. 9)

CD: 58

CD: 60

___ God.___

stars in the sky and You know them by_____ name._____

You are a - maz - ing_____ God._____

_____ In - com - p'ra - ble,___ un -

chang - a - ble,___ You see the depths of my heart and You

SCENE 8

SHARK: Thanks for all your help. Would you mind if I hung out with you guys? I'm gettin' a little tired of the Goliaths.

CARL: Sure thing, Dude. You can hang out with us anytime.

RANGER: Tyler, can you introduce me to our new friend?

TYLER: Sure thing, Ranger Clark. This is Shark…

SHARK *(interrupting)*: He means Albert Thompson, but you can call me Bert. *(shakes hands with RANGER CLARK)*

JAMES: He's our friend from school.

NED: Glad to have you, Bert.

SHARK: Thanks everyone. You guys are the best!

NARRATOR *(moves to center stage)*: Are you lost? Are you afraid? Do you have bullies in your life? If you trust in Jesus, He will live inside you and answer every need you could possibly have in life. *(music begins)* Just obey what He asks you to do. Come, be a part of His family. Open up your heart right now. Just remember, Jesus, the First Action Hero is just a prayer away, ready to give you His help. Come on everyone! Power up to Jesus!

First Action Heroes Finale

includes

All Hail the Power of Jesus' Name
There Is Power in the Blood
Indescribable
The First Action Hero

Arr. by John DeVries

*"All Hail the Power of Jesus' Name"

96

98

104

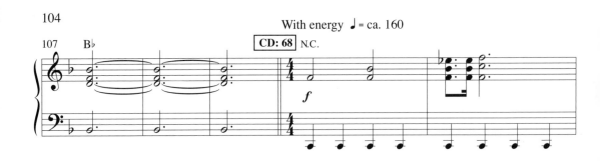

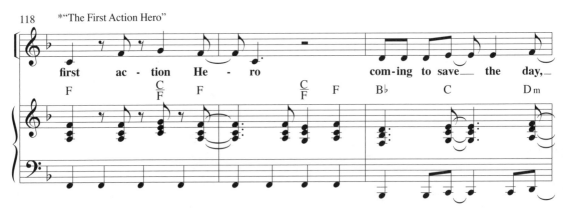

Curtain Call

includes

All Hail the Power of Jesus' Name
There Is Power in the Blood
The First Action Hero

Arr. by John DeVries

PLEASE NOTE: Copying of this product is NOT covered by CCLI licenses. For CCLI information call 1-800-234-2446.

*"There Is Power in the Blood"

112

PRODUCTION NOTES

Setting

The action occurs in Hero Park. There should be a giant hero comic book exhibit that consists of 5 comic book covers. (David, Esther, Joshua, Joseph, and Jesus). There should be park benches and street lights. Accent the stage with imitation trees and other foliage. The backdrop should be a dark city landscape. You should leave gaps in the landscape for the action heroes to enter and exit. The First Action Hero logo can be projected on a screen as if a city billboard. Many of these pieces are provided in the First Action Heroes Directors Resource Notebook or DVD including a backdrop design, art pieces, JPEG images, as well as complete construction ideas.

Casting Ideas

This musical is perfect for any size choir. You may perform the musical as written and utilize only the main characters if you have a smaller choir. If your choir is large, you may want to divide parts or add solos. Be creative. Giving every child some kind of special part will encourage attendance and participation. Pray for God to lead you to the right decisions.

Narrator	_____
Ranger Clark/Captain Super	_____
Ned/The Bible Boy Wonder	_____
Shark	_____
Snake	_____
Gang of Goliaths	_____
	_____
	_____
	_____
Tyler	_____
Carl or Carlos	_____
James or Jamar	_____
Jenna	_____
Tori	_____
David	_____
Esther	_____
Joseph	_____
Joshua	_____

Specialty Movement

To move or not to move?

In an effort to supply the needs of all our churches, we are providing you with choreography for this children's choir musical. We realize that according to various denominations, this may or may not be appropriate for your church. We encourage you to seek leadership from the Lord and your church leaders as you make your decision.

Note: The movement for the Specialty Movement Team is found in "The First Action Heroes" Resource Notebook or on "The First Action Heroes" DVD.

"The First Action Heroes" Movement Team

_____

_____

_____

_____

Cast and Costume

Actors

Narrator - should wear a "The First Action Heroes" T-shirt and jeans and sit on a stool

Ranger Clark - should wear a park ranger type costume.

Captain Super/Ranger Clark - can become Captain Super or he could be played by another child. Captain Super should wear a Super Hero Costume with silver pants and shirt with a Giant "A" on the front along with a red cape and a mask.

Ned - should also be dressed as an assistant ranger.

The Bible Boy Wonder/Ned - could become The Bible Boy Wonder or could be played by another child. The Bible Boy Wonder should wear a Super Hero Costume with silver pants and shirt with a Giant "B" on the front along with a blue cape and a mask. He should also carry a Bible.

Shark, Snake and other Goliaths - should wear gang style clothes with bandanas and leather jackets. They should carry spray paint cans.

Tyler, Carl (or Carlos), James (or Jamar) Jenna, Tori and Tyler - should wear "The First Action Heroes" T-shirt and jeans.

David, Esther, Joseph and Joshua - should wear a shiny Biblical costume made of gold or silver fabric.

Each character should have the following unique costume decoration:

    David - A bright yellow cape and a sling-shot with rock.

    Esther - A bright pink cape and a crown.

    Joseph - A cape of many colors, a bag of grain and possibly a crown.

    Joshua - A bright green cape and a trumpet.

Choir could wear "The First Action Hero" T-shirts and assorted colors of capes tied around their necks. To purchase these T-shirts, contact:

    Personalized Gifts & Apparel
    Tom Roland, Owner
    800.898.6170
    615.822.3452
    Website: www.pg4u.com
    Email: info@pg4u.com

OR you can download the T-shirt art from the Lillenas website at www.lillenas.com to create your own shirt.

Specialty Movement Team

The Specialty Movement Team costuming is found in "The First Action Hero" Resource Notebook and DVD.

The Set Design

The following is the layout of the set.

City landscape with power point screen for billboard

Risers						Risers
	David	Esther	Jesus	Joseph	Joshua	
		(Comic Book Covers)				

	Trees	Soloists		Soloists	Trees	
Park bench	x x				x x	Park bench
						Goliaths' Hide

Props

Sleeping bag
Backpack with bug repellent
Bible
2 Crowns
Trumpet
Ice Pack
Park Bench

Camping gear
Spray paint cans
Sling-shot and rock
Bag of grain
First Aid Kit
Pillow

The Directors Resource DVD contains a full compliment of images and scripture text that are designed for projection during your program. A listing is available at www.lillenaskids.com

Solos

Overture	No Solos
The First Action Hero	No Solos
Quest for Power	Captain Super Solo on verses 1& 2
Trust Is a Must	No Solos Use a small group for the 3-part harmony
Courage Conquers Fear	Solo on verse 2 Create an echo group for the bridge.
You're Forgiven	Solo on verses 1 & 2
Tell Me What Ya Know About Joshua Joshua Fought the Battle of Jericho	Solo on verses 1 & 2 Optional Solo on verses 1 & 2
He Is the Love	No Solos Create an echo group for the chorus
Indescribable	Solo on verses 1 & 2

First Action Heroes Finale
   All Hail the Power of Jesus' Name
   There Is Power in the Blood
 	
   Indescribable
   The First Action Hero
	
	No Solos
	Solo on verses 1 & 2
	Create an echo group for the chant.
	No Solos
	No Solos

Curtain Call	No Solos

Microphone Needs
It would be best to have a cordless lavaliere microphone for each main character. Hand-held microphones can be used as a substitute. Place two solo microphones on stands stage left and stage right to accommodate the solos.

Scripture References

Overture		Romans 1:16
Song 1	The First Action Hero	John 14:6
Song 2	Quest for Power	Psalm 147:5
Song 3	Trust Is a Must	Proverbs 3:5-6
Song 4	Courage Conquers Fear	1 Corinthians 16:13
Song 5	You're Forgiven	Colossians 3:13
Song 6	Tell Me What Ya Know About Joshua	Deuteronomy 27:10
Song 7	He Is the Love	1 John 4:7
Song 8	Indescribable	Psalm 8:1-9
Song 9	First Action Heroes Finale	Acts 1:8
Curtain Call		Psalm 150:1-6